Dec 2020

# Zoom In on
# Native American Leaders

# Chief Joseph

Jennifer Strand

**abdopublishing.com**

Published by Abdo Zoom™, PO Box 398166, Minneapolis, Minnesota 55439. Copyright © 2018 by Abdo Consulting Group, Inc. International copyrights reserved in all countries. No part of this book may be reproduced in any form without written permission from the publisher. Abdo Zoom™ is a trademark and logo of Abdo Consulting Group, Inc.

Printed in the United States of America, North Mankato, Minnesota
052017
092017

Cover Photo: De Lancey Gill/Frank and Frances Carpenter Collection/Library of Congress
Interior Photos: De Lancey Gill/Frank and Frances Carpenter Collection/Library of Congress, 1; North Wind Picture Archives, 4, 5, 10, 13, 14, 16–17; Robert Crum/Shutterstock Images, 6–7; Washington State Historical Society, 7; E. A. Burbank/Library of Congress, 9; Dr. Edward H. Latham/Library of Congress, 11; Rudolph B. Scott/Library of Congress, 12; G. M. Holland/Library of Congress, 15; Shutterstock Images, 18–19; National Photo Company Collection/Library of Congress, 19

Editor: Emily Temple
Series Designer: Madeline Berger
Art Direction: Dorothy Toth

**Publisher's Cataloging-in-Publication Data**
Names: Strand, Jennifer, author.
Title: Chief Joseph / by Jennifer Strand.
Description: Minneapolis, MN : Abdo Zoom, 2018. | Series: Native American
   leaders | Includes bibliographical references and index.
Identifiers: LCCN 2017931229 | ISBN 9781532120220 (lib. bdg.) |
   ISBN 9781614797333 (ebook) | 9781614797890 (Read-to-me ebook)
Subjects: LCSH: Joseph, Nez Perce Chief, 1840-1904--Juvenile literature. | Nez
   Perce Indians--Kings and rulers--Biography--Juvenile literature. | Nez Perce
   Indians--Wars, 1877--Juvenile literature.
Classification: DDC 979.5004/092 [B]--dc23
LC record available at http://lccn.loc.gov/2017931229

# Table of Contents

4

**Chief** Joseph was a leader of the Nez Perce **tribe**.

He tried to protect his people. He and his people **retreated** to escape fighting.

# Early Life

Joseph was born in 1840. He grew up in the Wallowa Valley. It is in Oregon.

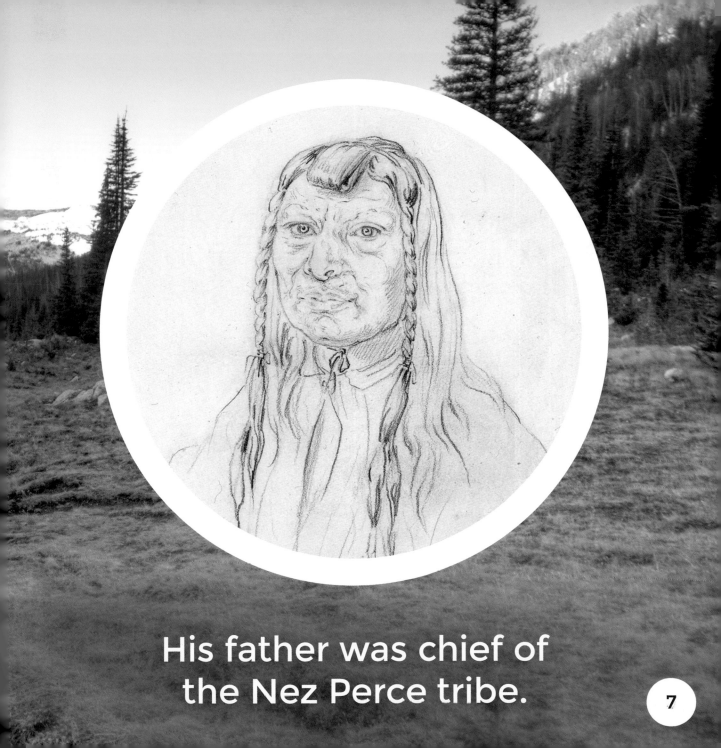

His father was chief of
the Nez Perce tribe.

# Leader

In 1871 Joseph became chief. Many US **settlers** were moving west. Some took land from the Native Americans.

In 1877 the US government tried to make the Nez Perce people leave their land.

At first Chief Joseph agreed.
But fighting broke out.

Chief Joseph wanted to protect his people.

So he tried to lead them to Canada. The Nez Perce walked for more than one thousand miles.

But the tribe did not make it there. The US army surrounded them.

On October 5, 1877, Chief Joseph agreed to end the tribe's retreat.

The US government sent the Nez Perce to a **reservation**. It was far from their homeland. Many tribe members got sick and died.

Chief Joseph asked if his tribe could return to its land but the government said no.

In 1885 the tribe was moved to a new reservation. Chief Joseph continued to speak out for his people. He died in 1904.

He is remembered as a great leader to the Nez Perce.

# Chief Joseph

**Born:** 1840, the exact date is not known

**Birthplace:** Wallowa Valley, Oregon Territory

**Known For:** Chief Joseph was a Nez Perce leader. When settlers took the tribe's land, he tried to lead his people to Canada.

**Died:** September 21, 1904

# Key Dates

**1840:** Chief Joseph is born. He is known as Young Joseph.

**1871:** Young Joseph becomes chief. During this time, many settlers are moving into Nez Perce land.

**1877:** Chief Joseph leads his people on a retreat to Canada. US troops capture them and send the tribe to a reservation in Oklahoma.

**1885:** The Nez Perce are moved to a reservation in Washington.

**1904:** Chief Joseph dies on September 21.

# Glossary

**chief** – the leader of a group of people.

**reservation** – an area of land in the United States that is set aside for Native Americans to live.

**retreat** – moving away from enemy soldiers to avoid fighting.

**settler** – a person who goes to live in a new place.

**tribe** – a group of people who share the same culture and beliefs.

# Booklinks

For more information on **Chief Joseph**, please visit abdobooklinks.com

## Zoom In on Biographies!

Learn even more with the Abdo Zoom Biographies database. Check out **abdozoom.com** for more information.

# Index